Buddha

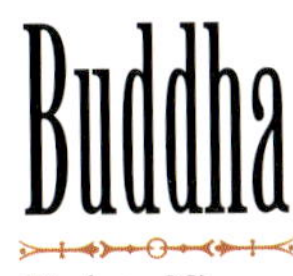

Birth to Nirvana

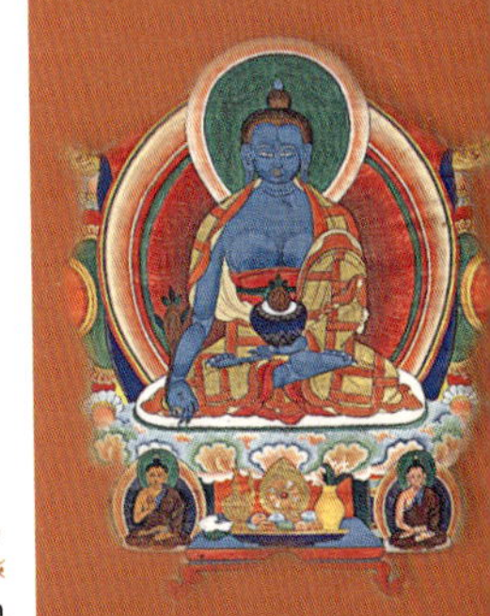

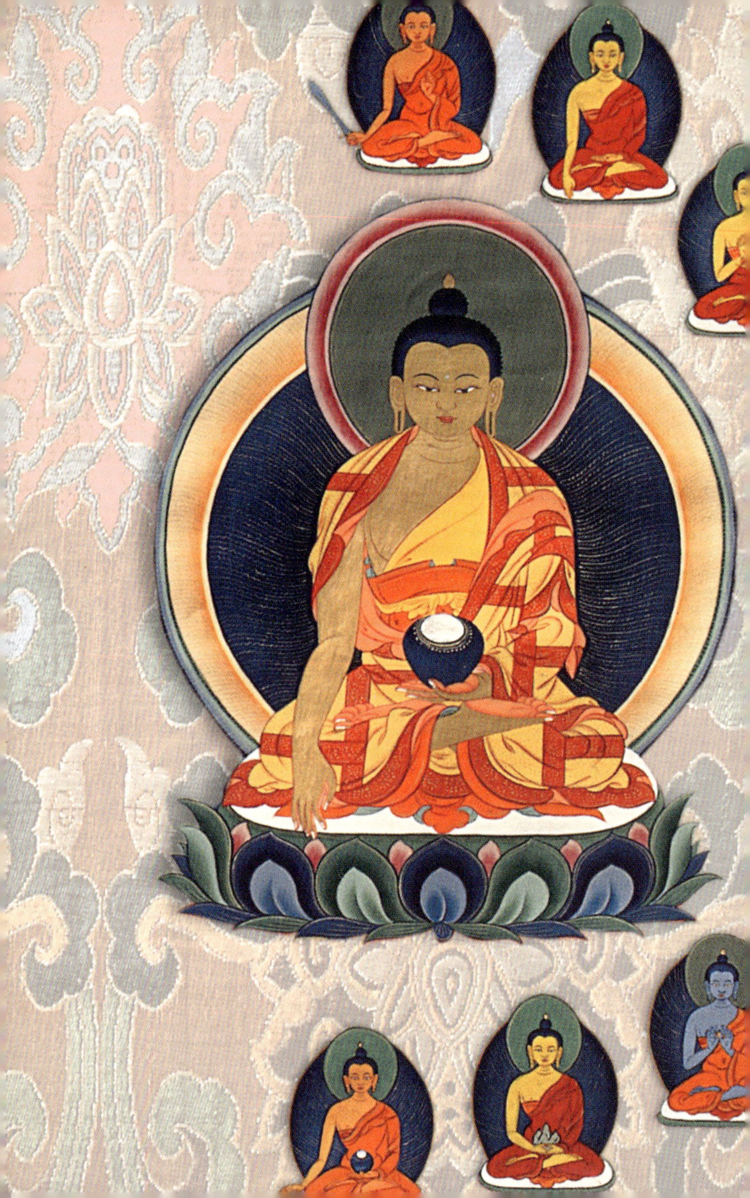

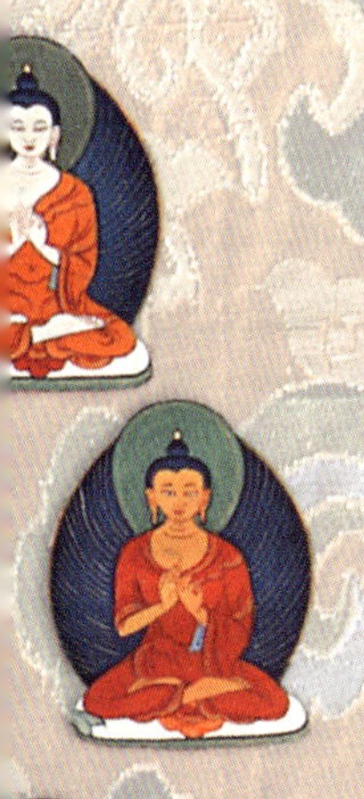

Buddha

Birth to Nirvana

Text: Jitendra Pant

Lustre Press
Roli Books

The thirty–year–old man, who was married and had sired a son, was returning to his palace rooms. A party had been going on and had left grotesque detritus in its wake. Beautiful dancing girls lay dishevelled and dehumanised; one yawned, another dribbled saliva from her open mouth. The empty casks of pleasure, drunk to the full, presented a macabre similitude of death, a degrading cloak of lifelessness to what had been gay and riotous moments ago.

The man paused and was filled with disgust. The moonlit-scene of human waste helped confirm his decision. He hurried on to his sleeping chamber. His wife lay sleeping, their son by her side. For a moment, he hesitated: should he wake her up? He decided otherwise, fearing that their parting would be made harder. He called for his charioteer, asked for his horse and left palace life behind forever.

Thus was inaugurated an episode in religious history, and more importantly, in the record of man's search for his own spirit, that has few, if any, parallels. For the thirty-year-old was Siddhartha, the only son of Suddhodhana, king of the Sakya clan. Its importance was, however, not immediately evidenced. Later, Buddhist literature was to dub it the Great Renunciation.

At that time, it was not a shocking event. When Siddhartha was born (around the middle of sixth century B.C.), his greatness had already been hinted at. His mother dreamt that a six-tusked elephant had placed a lotus inside her. Then, a holy man predicted that the infant would become a great teacher. The king tried unsuccessfully to thwart destiny, cocooning Siddhartha behind the palace walls with a carefree life of pleasure. Yet, life poked its head in or stared Siddhartha in the face when he went out, visiting the city with his charioteer. The keen balance between life and death, veiled so carefully, tilted to expose the heart of human suffering. Unlike almost everybody else, young Siddhartha could not remain immune to this, could not accept living as if life had not end.

His experiences of this troubled period are telescoped under what are called the Four Noble Sights: that of an old person, an incurably ill man, a corpse, and an ascetic. They are a full account, in shorthand, of human misery; a faithful representation of the puzzle that faced Siddhartha; and another hint of the way he would take to solve it.

Later, he likened the problems to four mountains coming at one with unstoppable speed, leaving neither space nor time for manoeuvre or escape. He took seven years to fathom the way out.

First, he apparently went on the wrong track. Under two teachers, he learnt to enter states of consciousness that were imperturbable and left him with much calmness. Yet, they were more like painkillers and hardly near the cure. Unimpressed,

Siddhartha left the teachers, declining their offers to head their respective sects.

He then decided that the answer could not be found until bodily desires were overcome. So followed a period of self-mortification and bodily denial that cut as deep as the bone. The former prince's skin hung loose; his body was exposed to the vagaries of the seasons, and hunger and every other impulse was scorned. Five companions from the teachers' sects were his co-sufferers. Then one day during meditation, he felt a cool breeze soothe his body and ease his mind. In a flash, he saw what was

During ritual worship, hand gestures add to the mood.

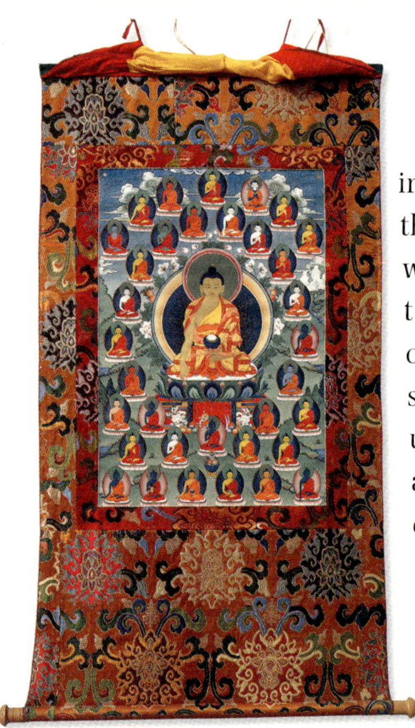

A *thangka*, a sacred Buddhist painting, depicts Buddha's postures.

incorrect about starving the body of its needs: he was seeking to cast aside the body in pursuit of the final answer when such separation was unnatural. The body and mind, Siddhartha concluded, were one and could not be twisted apart.

He abandoned the old method, the worn-out and wearing-out trail of letting the body rot. His companions parted ways as they saw Siddhartha accept nourishment from children, feeling he had deserted the ideal towards which they had started out. But Siddhartha was not worried. His seven-year search was about to end as his body and mind regained strength and equipoise. He began to meditate again, looking deeply into his own feelings, disentangling reality from dogma. Then one night it happened. Siddhartha, 'the one who attains his aim', became the Buddha, the Awakened One.

He awoke from the grand dream of identification: that the body was him, that feelings were him, that the predispositions of mind were him, that consciousness was him. He woke up to an even greater theme: the co-dependence and sympathetic unity of all things, the impermanence of every atom in creation, the non-existence of any self – either internal or external.

The answer was finally there: the Buddha was not separate from the rest of creation. There was no death to fear or defeat, no birth to rejoice at or bemoan, no liberation to attain since there was no one to liberate. Put another way: if the universe was a paper drawing, it was a drawing from which one could not cut out any individual or entity. To do so would be to destroy it.

The doctrine of non-self, as it came to be called, was not a theory of no-self. It did not say that there was no self. It did not challenge the idea of a soul or *atman,* since the soul, the Godhood immanent in every man, was understood to have manifested as the world itself. Instead, the theory of non-self pointed to the insubstantiality or emptiness behind the idea of identity.

The Buddha's major departure was from Brahmanism. Brahmanical thinking had entangled the matter of enlightenment or liberation with a complicated system of gaining religious merit. The arrangement of society into castes, which grew rigid and degrading, further occluded the system. After some time, it was comprehensible only to the few who had engineered it and whom it upheld – the Brahmans. Gone was the spirit of intense enquiry, of poetic wonderment and of renunciation which found expression in the sacred texts such as the *Upanishads* and the *Vedas.*

Into the Buddha's welcoming arms went those who had till then been denied dignity and rights under the system, and those who made up the elite. Buddhism can thus be seen as a revolt against Brahman orthodoxy. But as far as the Buddha is concerned, he was a man who was in internal revolt rather than external rebellion. The analogy that he gave for his liberation is indicative of how he placed himself. Ignorance was his jailer, keeping him behind bars for lifetimes. Ignorance had led to deluded views, to wanting and grasping, to thwarted desire and negative feelings, to the impulse to hit and hurt. Now that he could see the jailer clearly, see how he bound him, he was free of him.

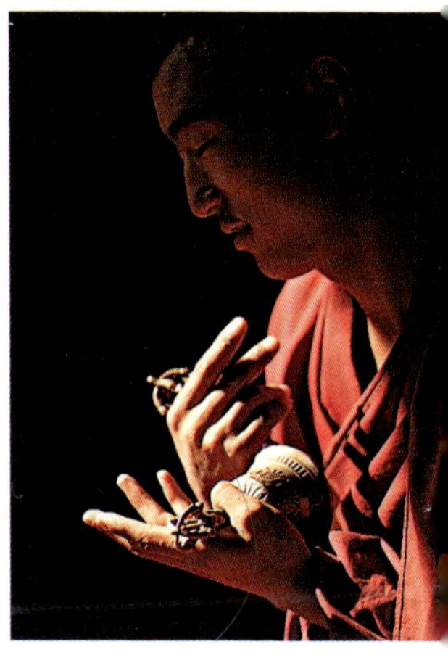

The *ghanta* (bell) and *dorje-vajra* (sceptre)

A deep appreciation of the butterfly-flittings of life, its iridescent and evanescent colours, its single beating heart came into being. With this came understanding and love, compassion and grace, insight, gratitude and healing. The universe was reinstated in the individual.

In its formulation that ignorance is what keeps us jailed, Buddhism and Hinduism reach a common ground. In the Hindu

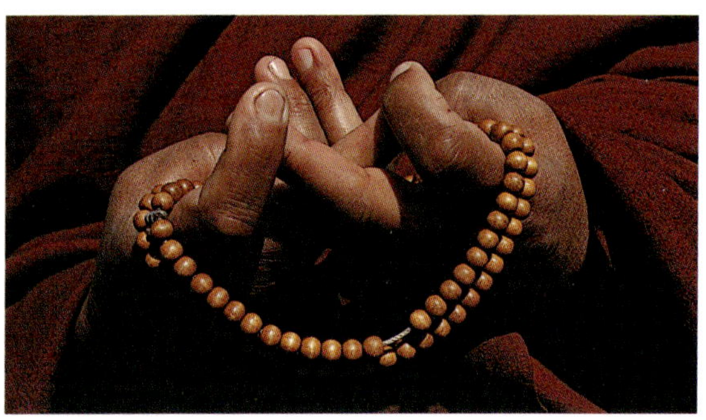

The rosary has 108 beads which are counted.

scriptures, *maya*, the veil of delusion that permeates the cosmos, is fathered by ignorance. It is an active hindrance in seeing the universe as a single entity, causing unified reality to be split into manifold expressions.

The Buddha with his view of interdependence and sympathetic unity also emphasised this point.

He advocated the middle way, one that charted the territory between sensual indulgence and self-abnegation, to solve the problem. An extremely simple logic formed the bedrock of his teachings. He postulated that life was filled with suffering, the scales of joy and sorrow tilting to favour happiness this instant and grief the next. Both emotions and events had no permanence. Yet, what caused such a burden of misery? In a word – desires. A vast territory of psychological ferment, of demands for appreciation and gratification, in fact, nothing less than the whole core of the human self, lay in the mind. With desire, the games of the mind began. Often man sang to desire's mesmerising tune without knowing why. It was in his ignorance that the tragedy lay.

The next step in the doctrine followed naturally: do away with desires. And the gates of abiding happiness and *nirvana* would be yours. But the Buddha differed from all others in the way he chose to end desire. The trick was not to avoid it or to get involved in a confrontation with it but to look deeply into its nature and causes. It was more a matter of cultivating an attitude of mindfulness towards desires rather than wilfully bludgeoning them into temporary submission. The Buddha even developed breathing exercises and routines to help nurture such awareness and sensitivity. Mindfulness let one taste the texture of life, unshackling the psychological effects – whether pleasurable or painful – of its experiences.

The first to walk the middle way with the Buddha were his five companions. They also formed his audience when he delivered his opening sermon at the Deer Park in Sarnath. So significant is the event considered that Buddhism has flagmarked it as *dharmachakraparivartan* or the Turning of the Wheel of Law. These five formed the nucleus around which the *sangha* (order) grew. With generous grants of land from noblemen and noblewomen, it established itself as what it was meant to be: a community of refuge. The Buddha gave to his order simplicity and humility. The monks and nuns were merely to do with two robes for a dress, a begging bowl, a fan and a needle. No other encumbrances were added. Food was obtained by begging, an exercise the Buddha believed helped nurture humility. It also kept

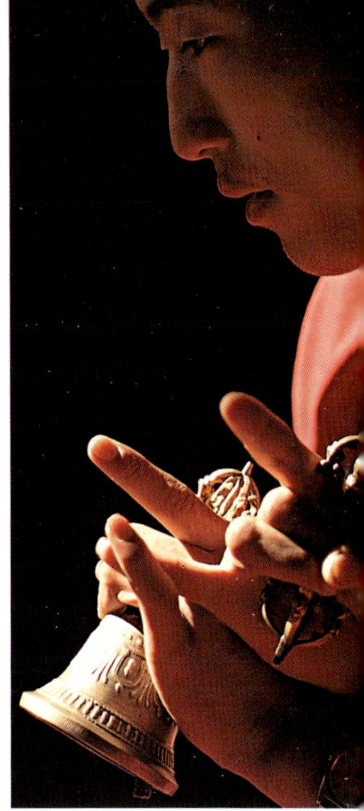

A monk rings the bell.

the *sangha* in contact with the rest of the community and lay disciples. Sermons by him and senior disciples guided the monks or *bhikkus*. In time, women entered the *sangha*. The inevitable discord associated with any large group took place. Unscrupulous schemes by sects to which Buddhism posed a threat tried to besmirch the Buddha. But is the sun shadowed by clouds? Unruffled and ever kind, he taught through these and they fell through.

At the age of eighty, after having a meal of sandalwood mushrooms at the home of a disciple, a blacksmith's son, the Buddha suffered an acute attack of dysentery. Still travelling on foot, he and the monks entered the forest near the entrance to a small village, Kushinagar. The *sal* trees were in full bloom and their red flowers carpetted the earth. The Buddha lay down to rest. It was a well-deserved one: he had been teaching for half a century. Once more he outlined the middle way and exhorted the monks around him to be diligent. Once more, he accepted a disciple. Then the lotus folded its petals amid a shower of red flowers.

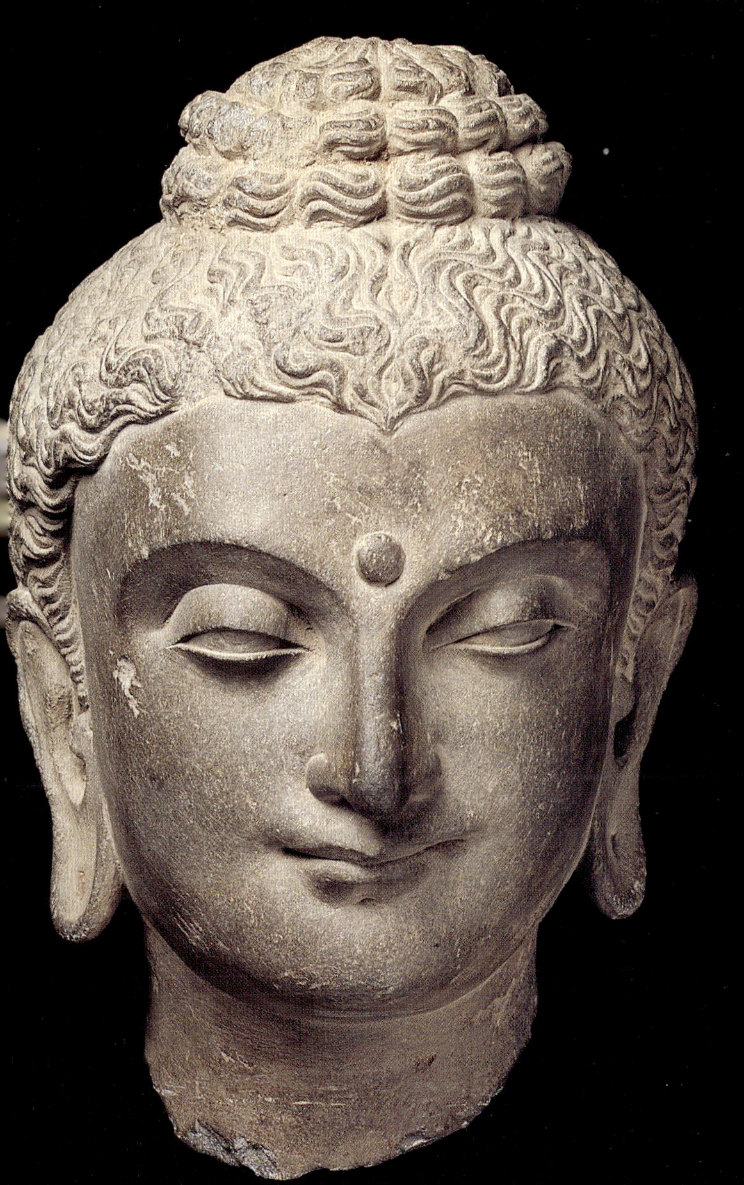

■ Buddha, the Enlightened. One

It took seven years for Siddhartha or The One Who Accomplishes His Aim to reach his goal and become Buddha.

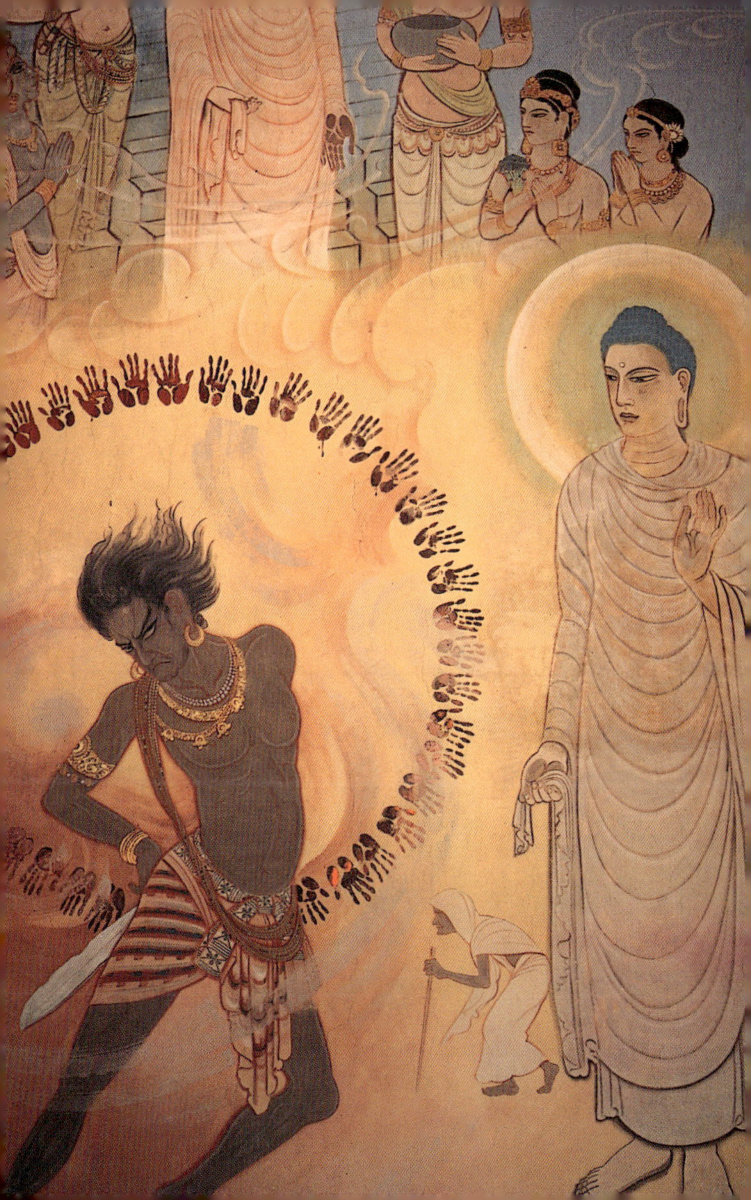

■ The conversion of Angulimal

A terrible murderer named Angulimal (one who wears a garland of fingers) had a change of heart after he met the Buddha. He was accpeted in the sangha and became the monk Ahimsaka.

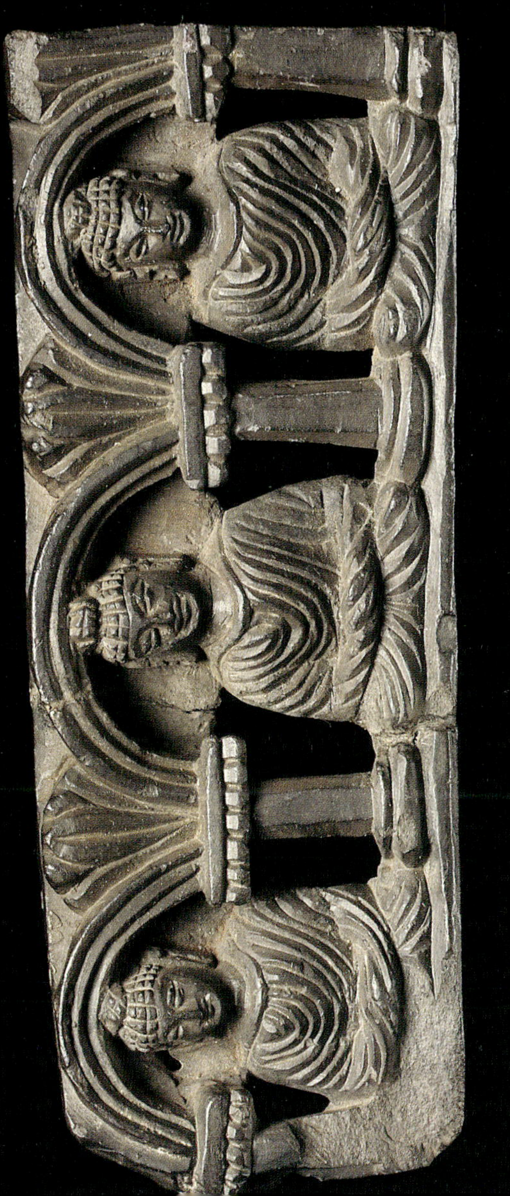

■ Three forms, one spirit

The Buddhas sit in identical lotus postures, the one deemed most suitable for meditation. Sculpted drapery was a feature of the Gandhara School of Art.

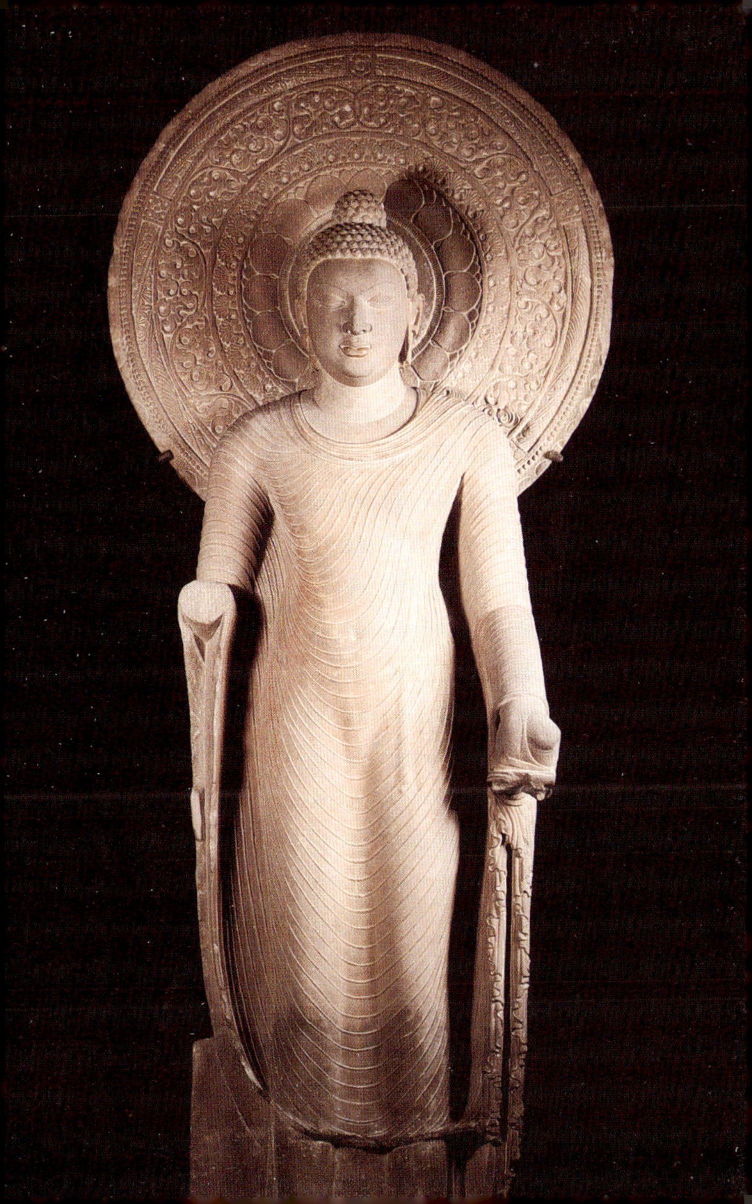

■ A standing Sakyamuni statue with a halo

The nimbus is symbolic of divinity; here it is a sign of the Gupta period of art with the Buddha wearing a monk's robe. This image is the largest known in this style.

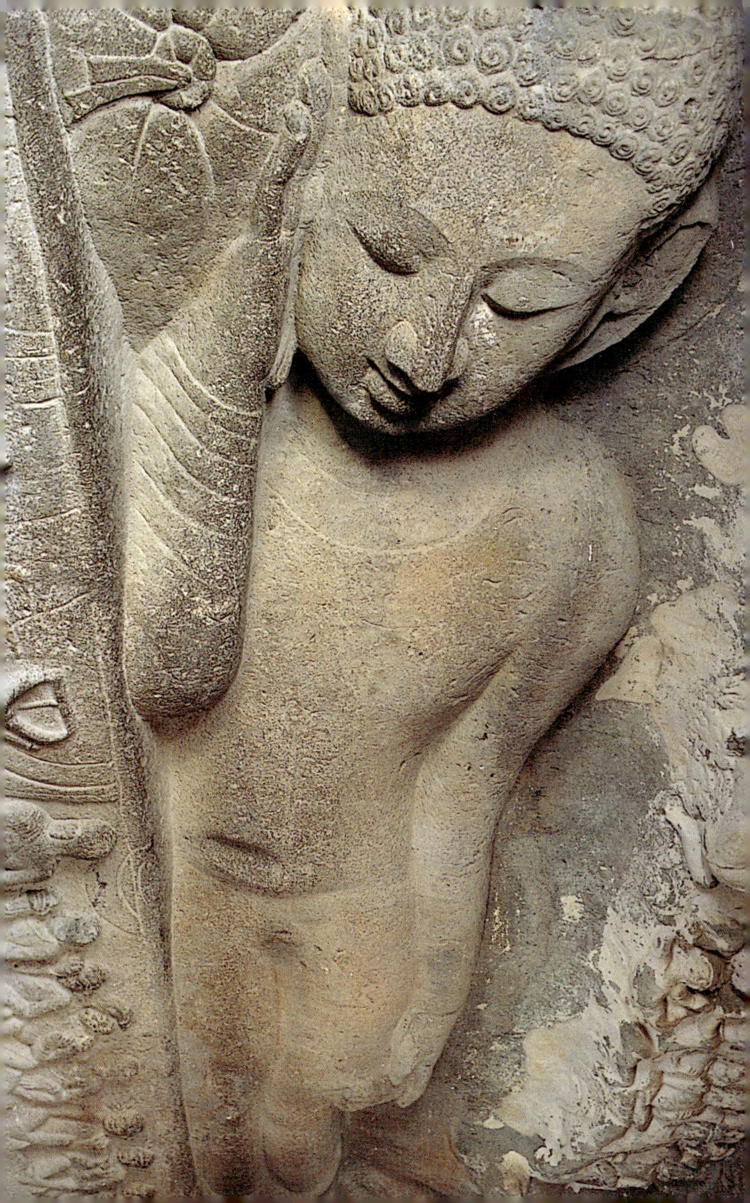

■ Buddha's *parinirvana*

At the age of eighty, the Buddha took ill after eating a dish of sandalwood mushrooms. He lay down among two sal trees and gave his last sermon.

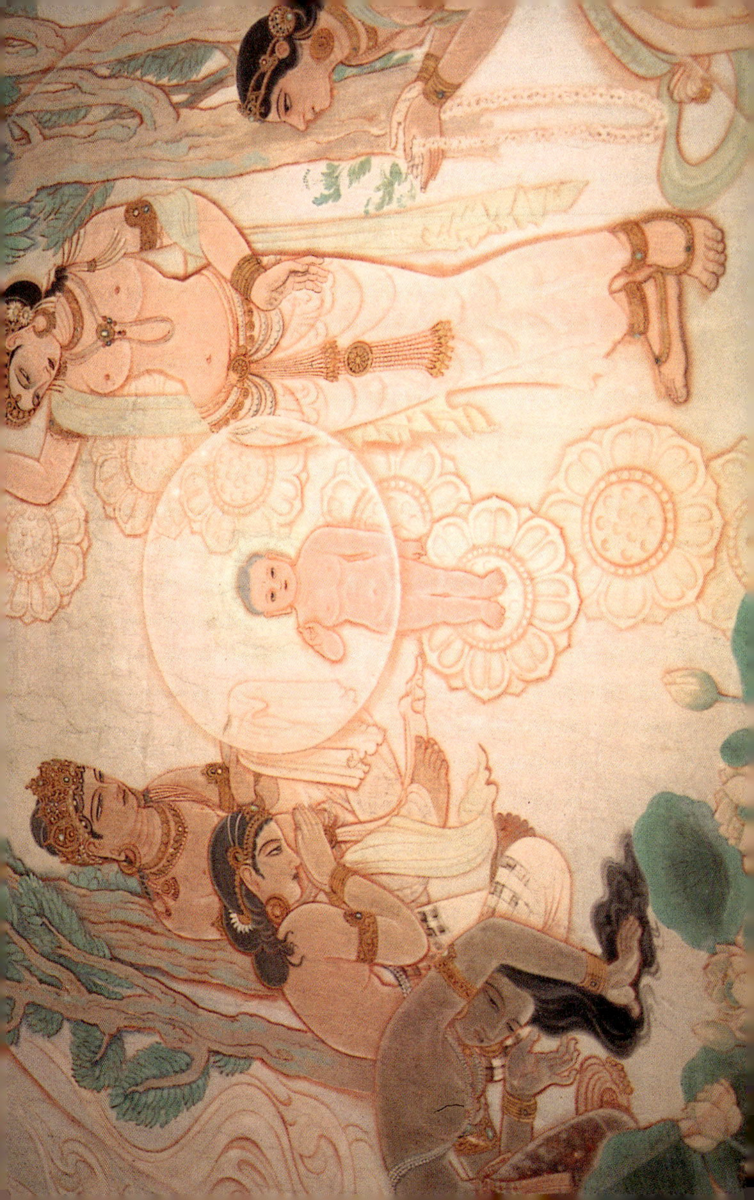

■ Homage to the little Buddha

The rich mythology surrounding the Buddha's birth sees him as a Bodhisattva who has come down from the heavens to take the last step towards enlightenment and bless the earth with the fragrance of his presence and the honey of his teachings.

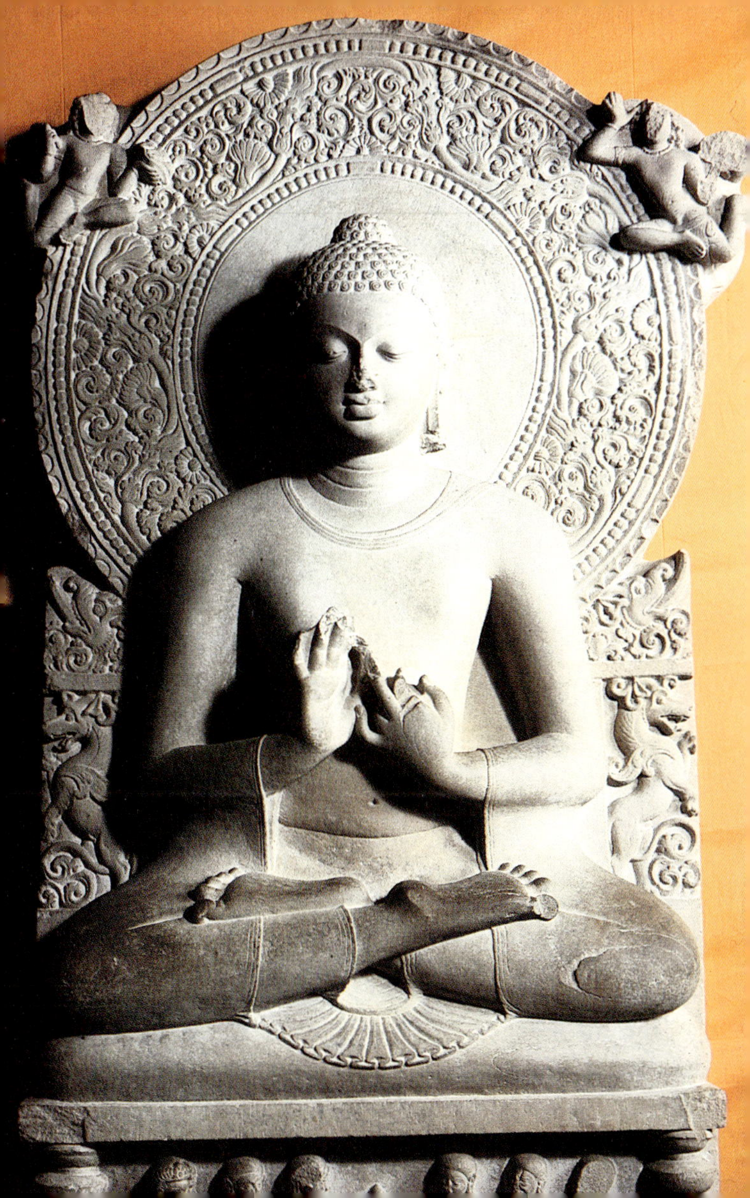

■ Buddha in the sermon *mudra* (pose)

After he attained enlightenment at the age of thirty-seven, the Buddha preached his first sermon at the Deer Park in Sarnath.

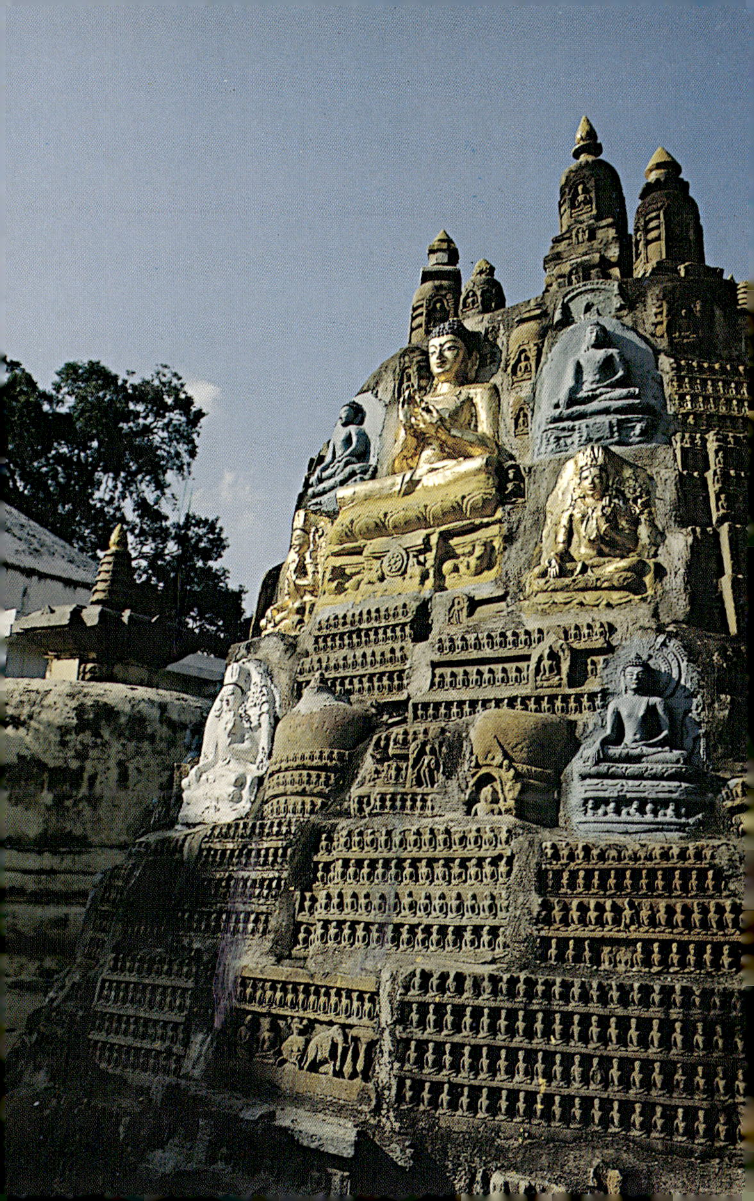

■ The Mahabodhi temple at Bodh Gaya

The second-century temple came up at the site of a shrine set up by King Ashoka near the bodhi tree. The temple's outer wall displays modern additions of the Buddha icon.

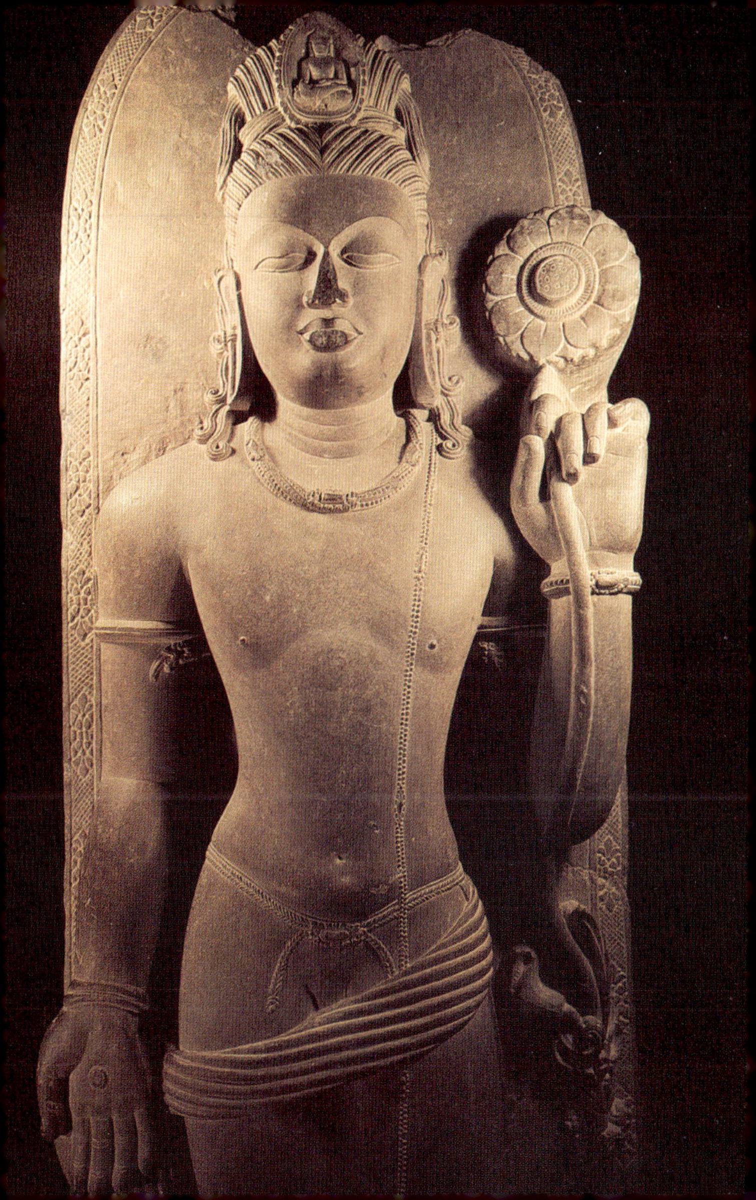

■ Avalokiteswara, the embodiment of compassion

The sandstone statue of the ninth century shows Avalokiteswara holding the rose-lotus. In his hair sits the transcendent Buddha Amitabha, whose emanation he is.

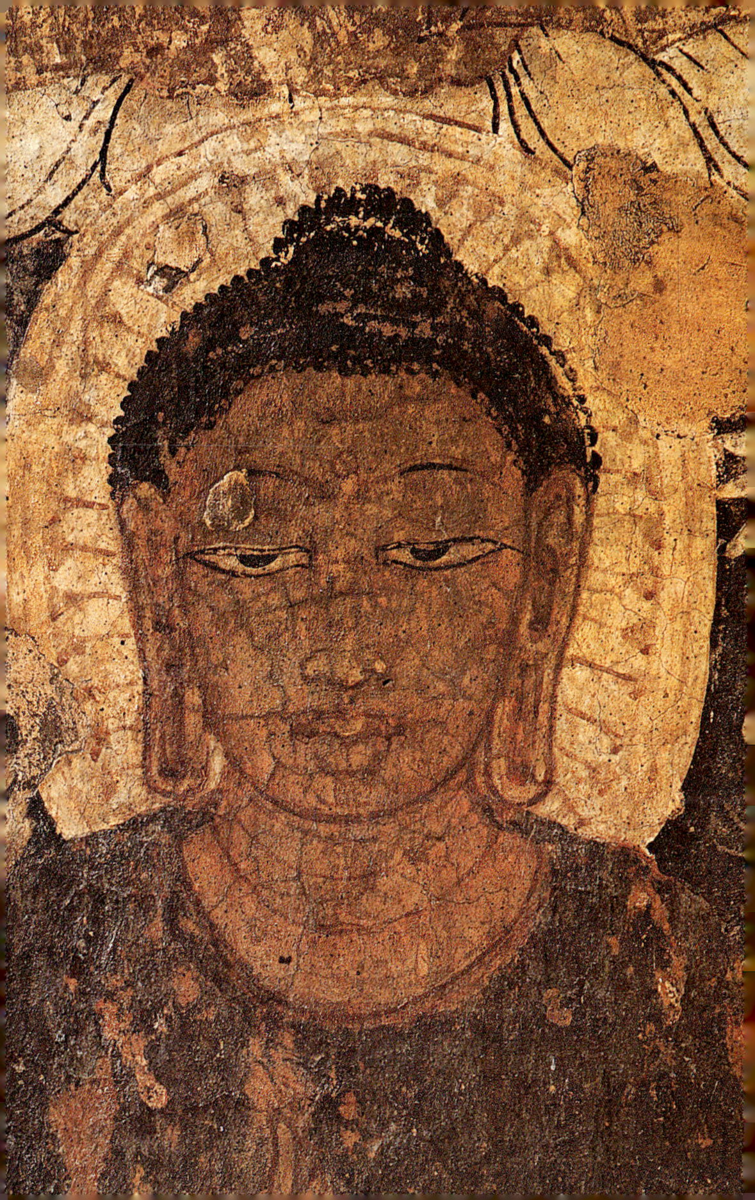

■ Buddha, the Awakened One

His journey of self-realisation started when he was thirty and he left his wife and son behind. After he singlehandedly achieved enlightenment, he taught ceaselessly for forty-seven years to become one of the world's greatest masters.

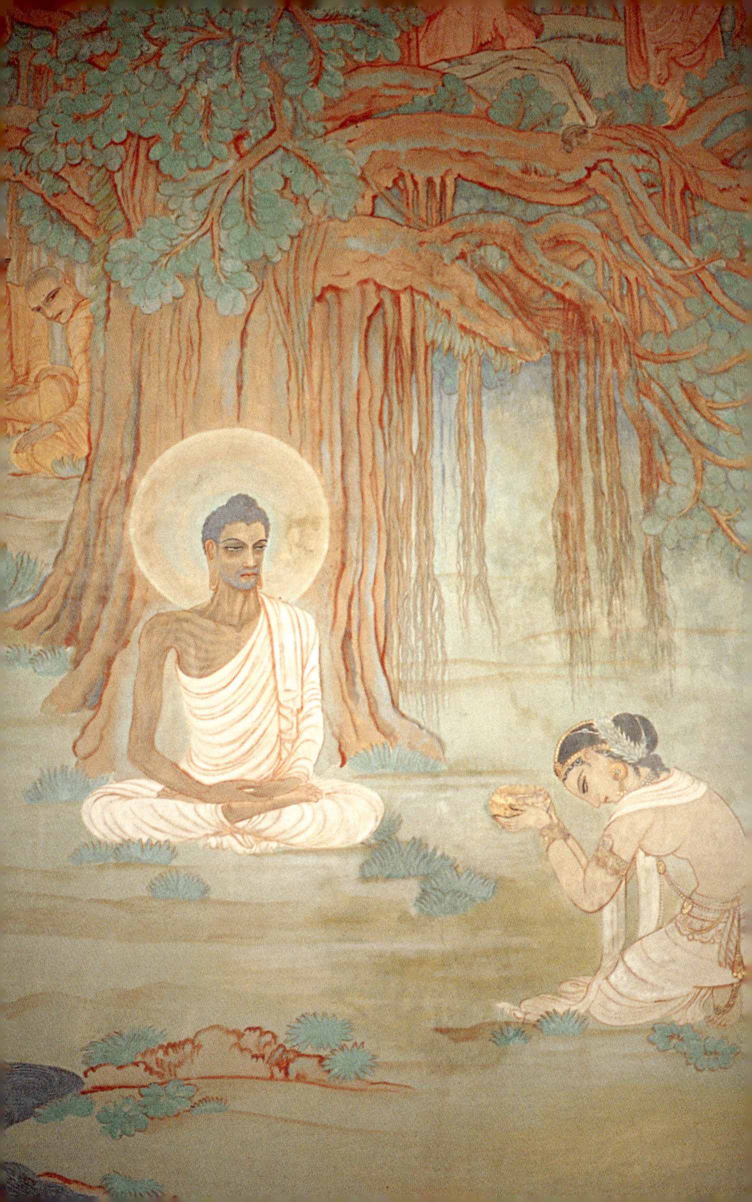

■ Sujata brings an offering for the Buddha.

Under the bodhi *tree, the Buddha attained nirvana. Liberation was a culmination of his seven-year pursuit for answers to the problems of life.*

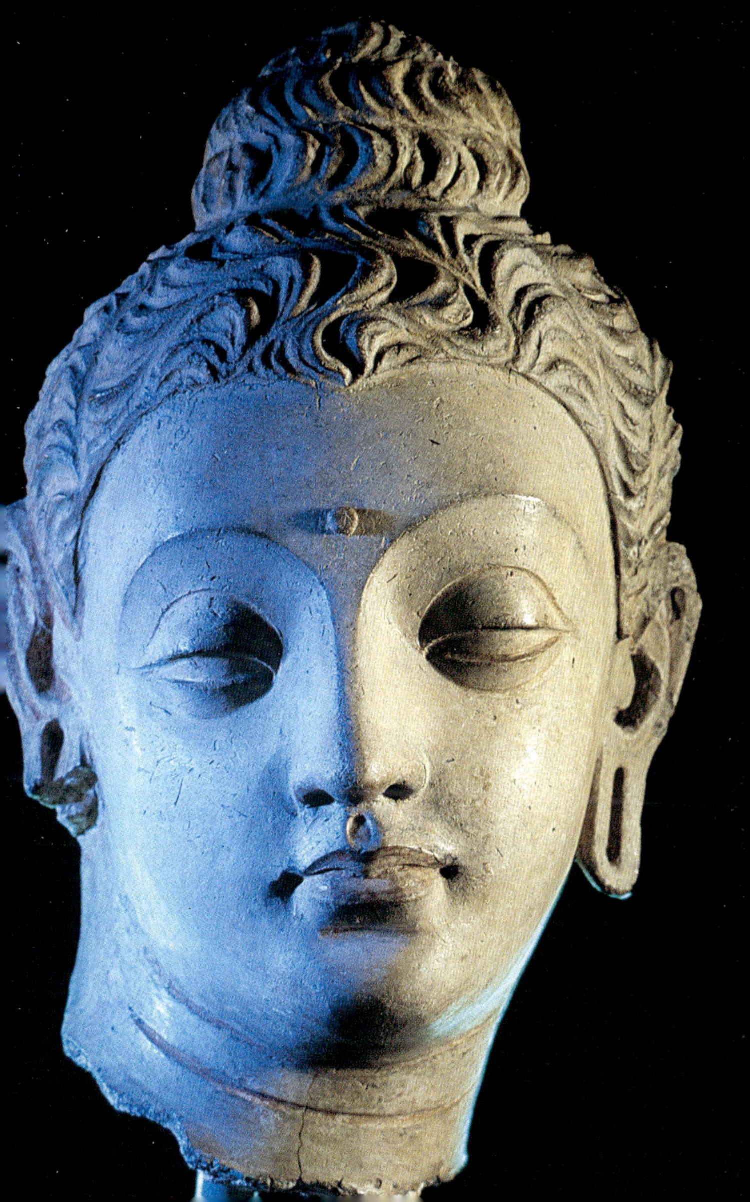

■ *Buddham Sharnam Gachami*

'I take refuge in the Buddha.': The idea of taking refuge (sharan) with a guru or spiritual master is a Hindu and Buddhist tradition. Forging a bond that cannot be severed by the relativity of life and death, the disciple puts his life before his master to be disposed of as per his master's will.

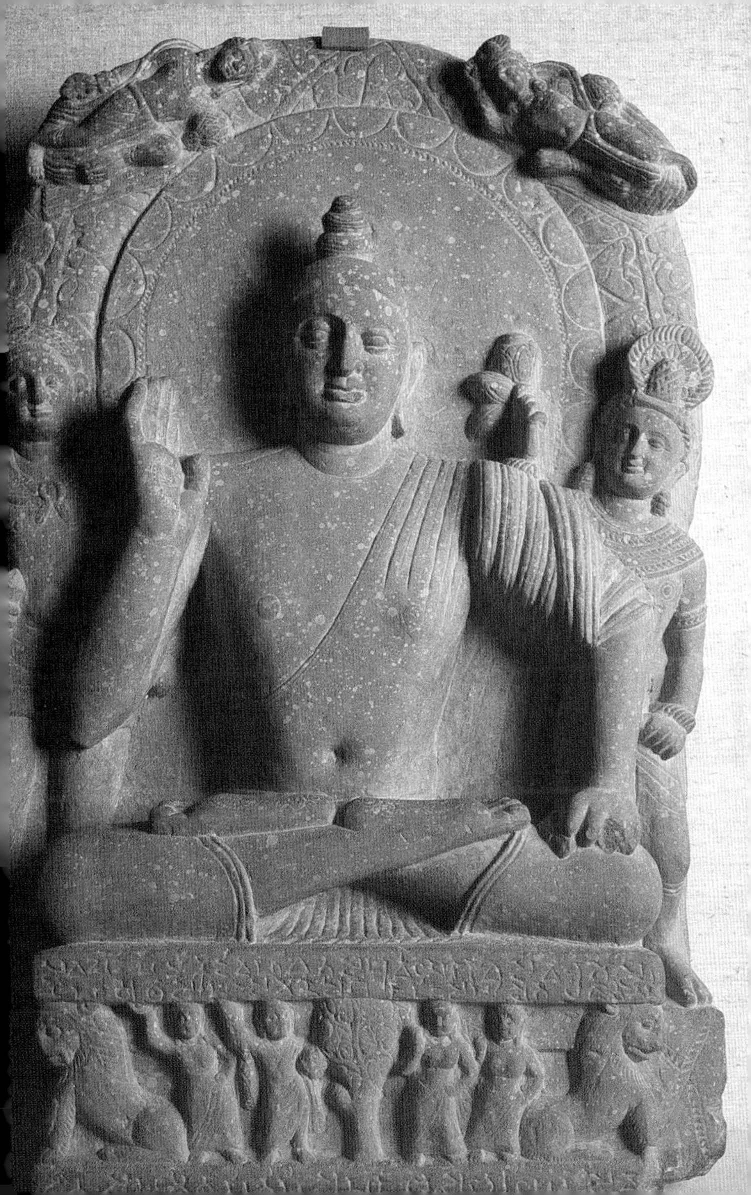

■ The *Abhaya Mudra*

'The Buddha seated under the pipal tree makes the sign (mudra) of fearlessness (abhaya) with his right hand. To the left is the lightning-bearer, the Bodhisattva Vayrapani; to the right, is perhaps an old version of Avalokiteswara.

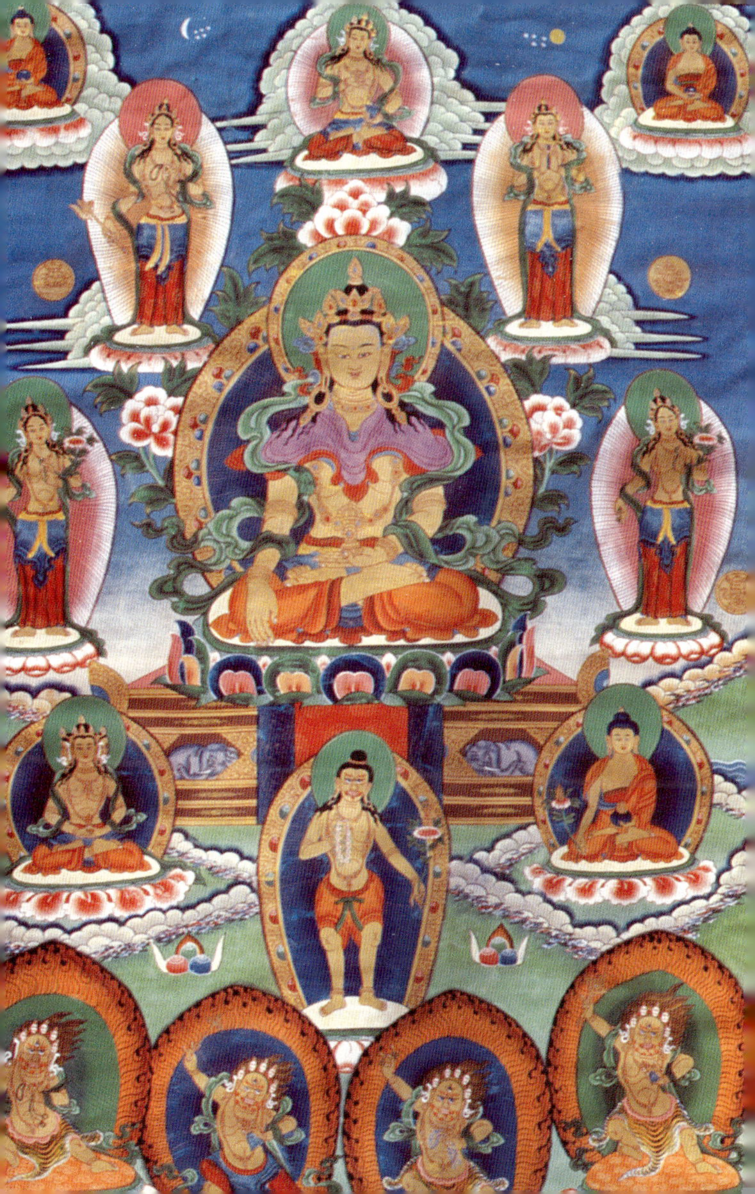

■ The Buddha and his incarnations

At the base of the thangka *are the wrathful deities, a characteristic of Tibetan Buddhism that was borrowed from Hindu tantra.*

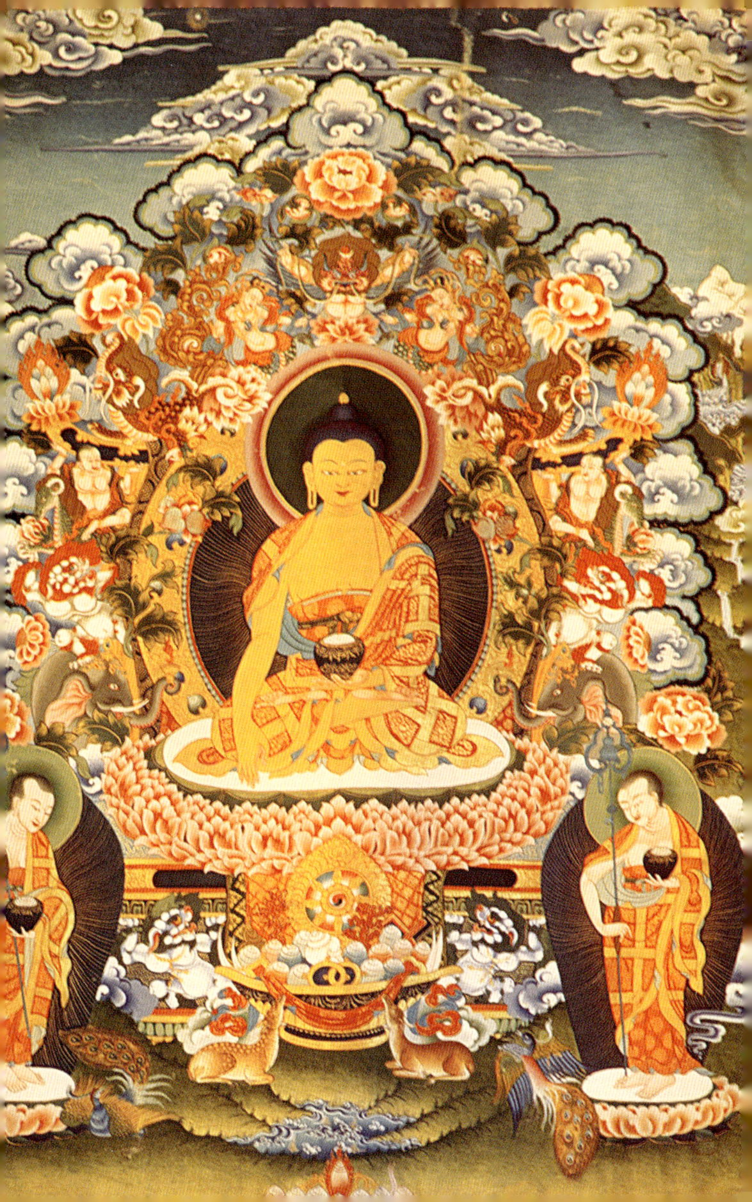

■ The Buddha with his disciples

Sariputra and Maudgalyayana (the figures at the lower corners of the painting) were the Sakyamuni's foremost disciples; his personal attendant and disciple for a great part of his life was, of course, the devoted Ananda.

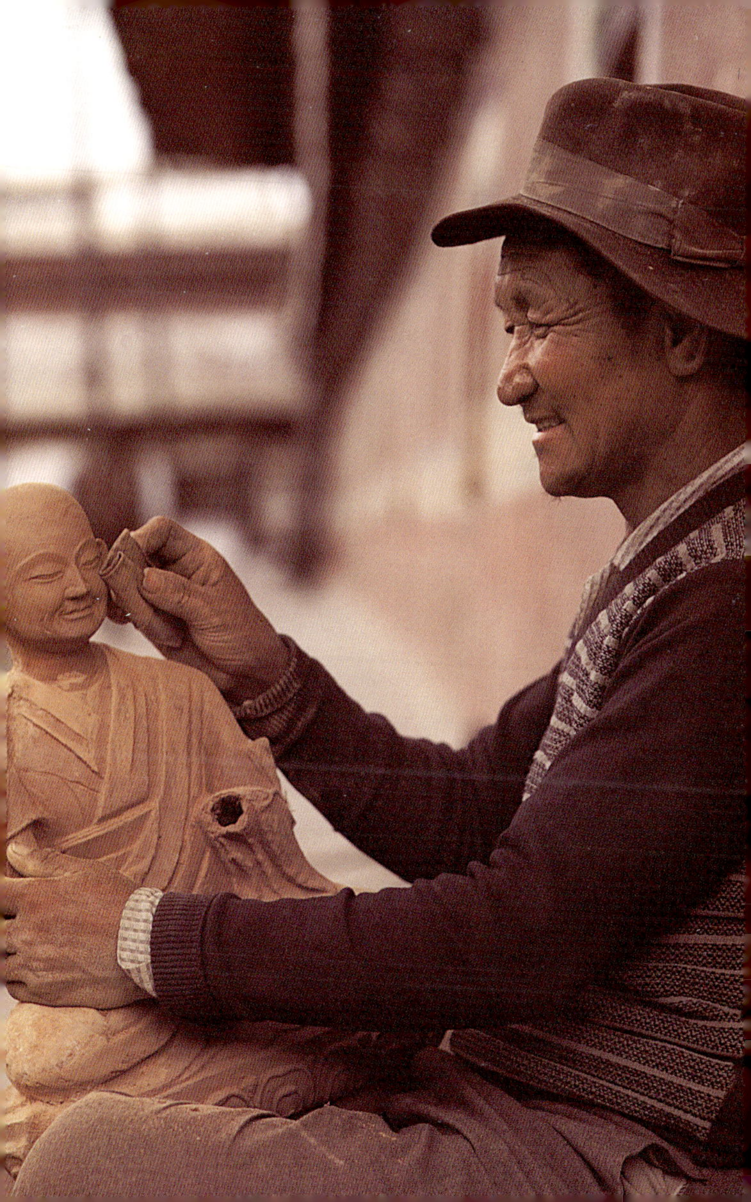

■ Manufacturing Buddhahood

A cheerful craftsman in a Tibetan bazaar shapes the ear of a smiling Bodhisattva. Customarily, Buddha's representations have long ears, a mark of his years of princely life. The extension in ear length came about, it is reasoned, because he wore earrings.

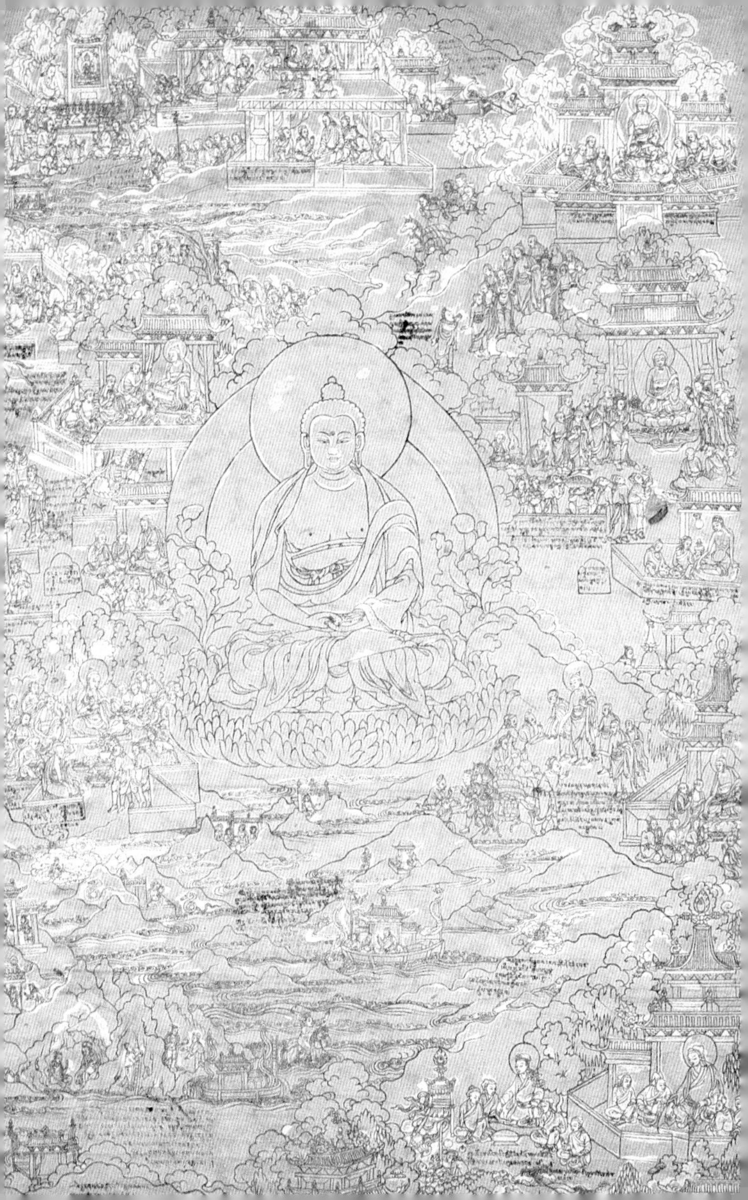

■ An uncoloured *thangka*

Without its colours the thangka *clearly shows the fine, painstaking detailing and brush work that goes into its making.*

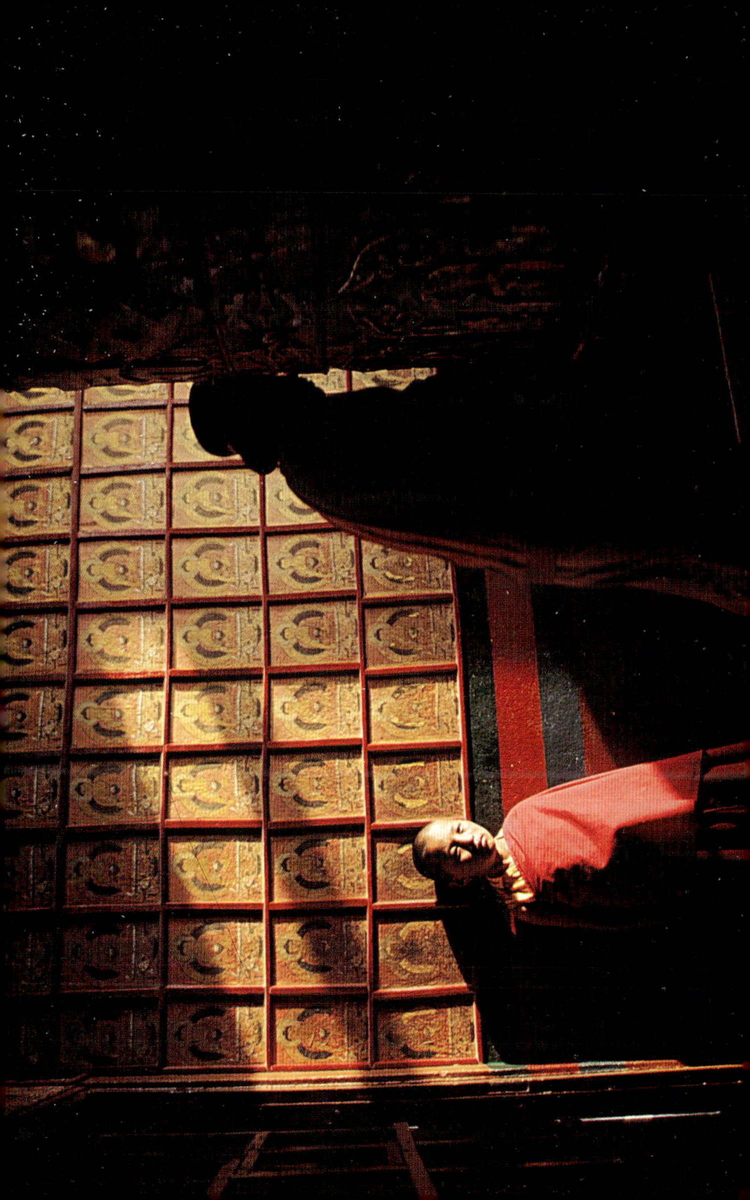

■ Wheel of life

The Sakyamuni looks on through innumerable faces as a young monk stands beside a big rotating prayer wheel. In Indian philosophy Samsara *is the ever-moving wheel of births and deaths. Desire is its motive force; suffering is its consequence.*

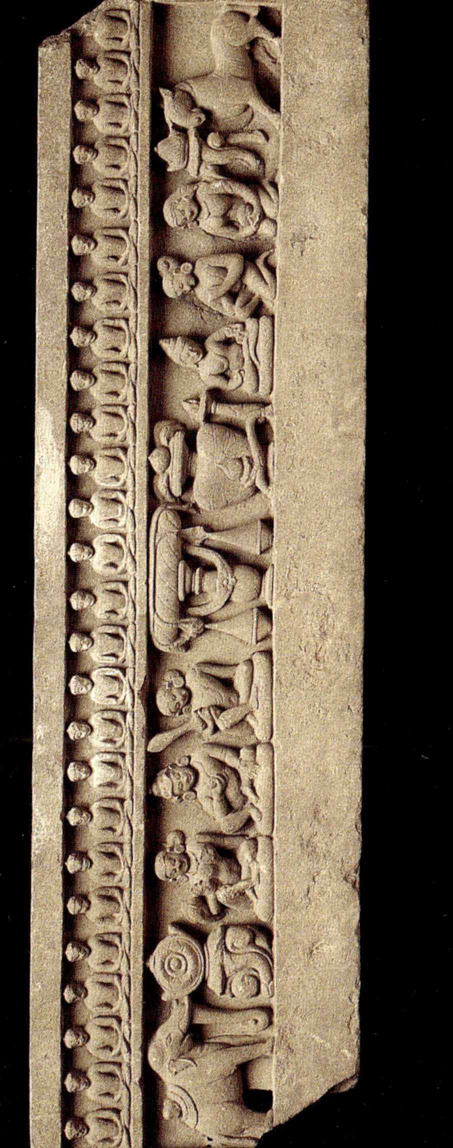

■ A sculpture in adoration of the Buddha

Sculpture has been a principal means of depicting religious life and momentous religious events in India. Pieces of sculpture outlive monarchs and their dynasties if not man's greed.

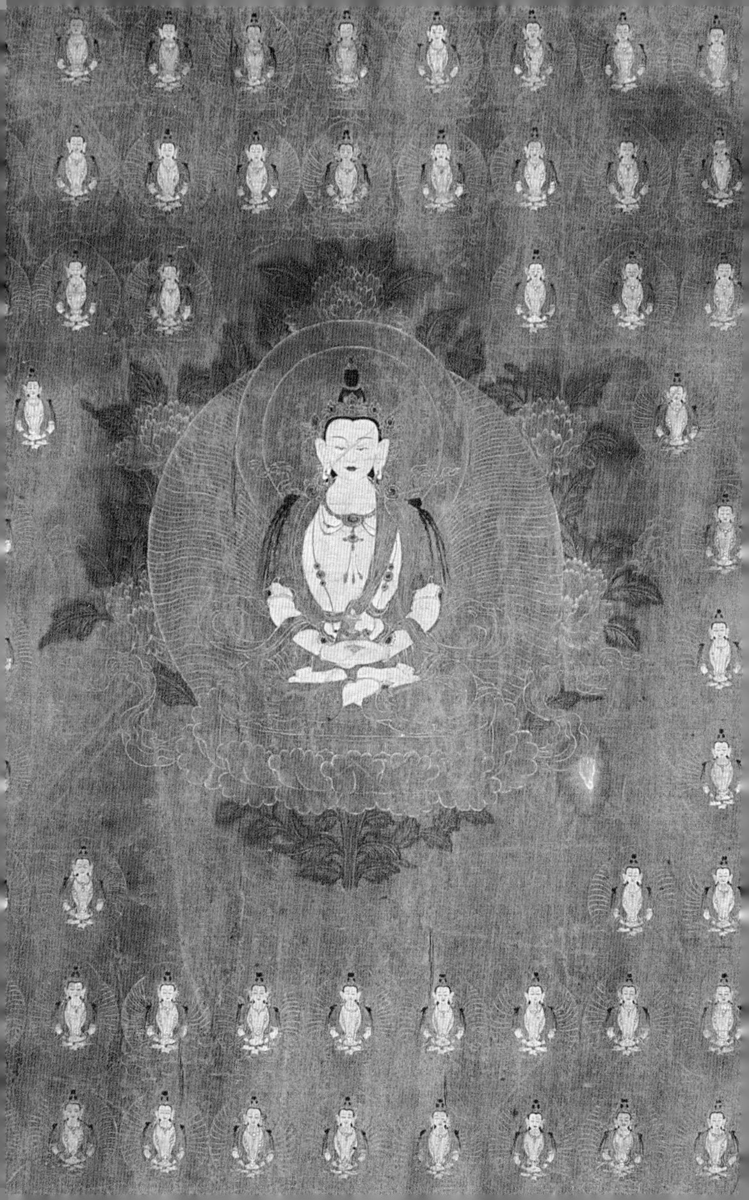

■ The *thangka* for longevity

Thangkas *are Buddhist scroll paintings on silk. They follow a complex system of iconography that details measurements for the drawn figures. This scroll shows the Amitayus or Buddha of Limitless Life.*

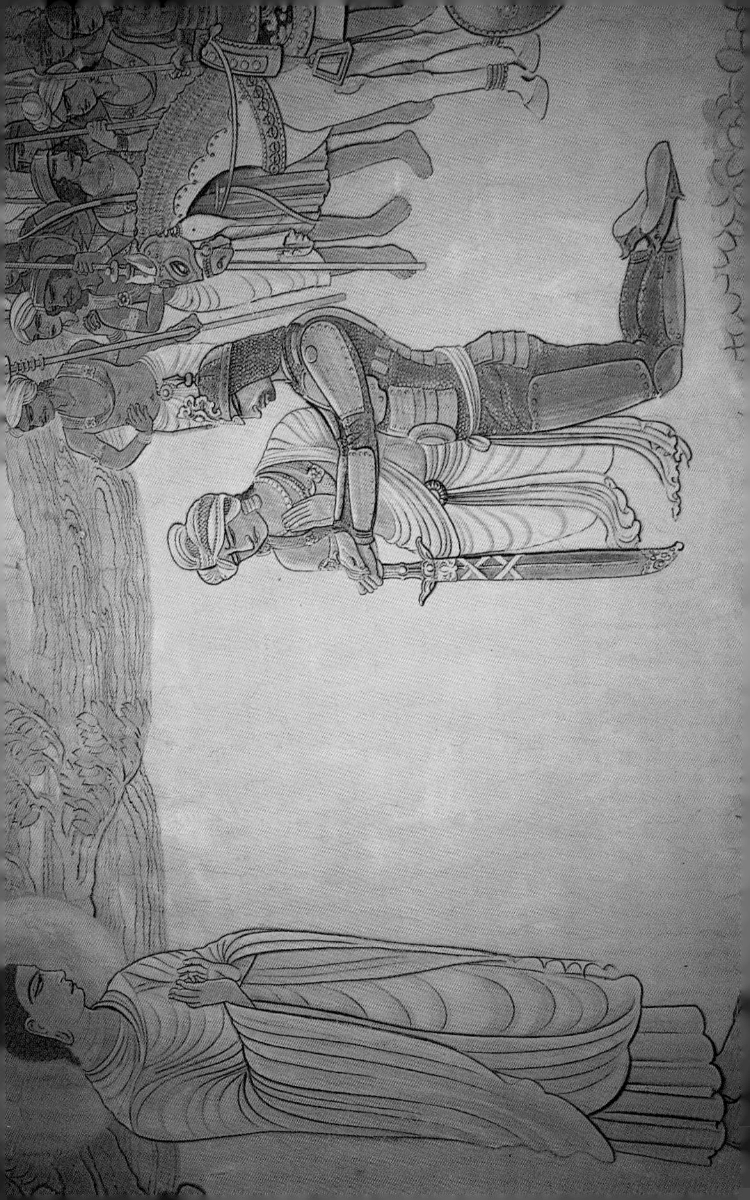

■ The king of men receives obeisance from a king.

The Buddha was a prince himself and his father was King Suddhodana. During the years of his penance he made friends with King Bimbisara. Later, he also accepted Ajatasatru, Bimbisara's patricidal son, as a disciple.

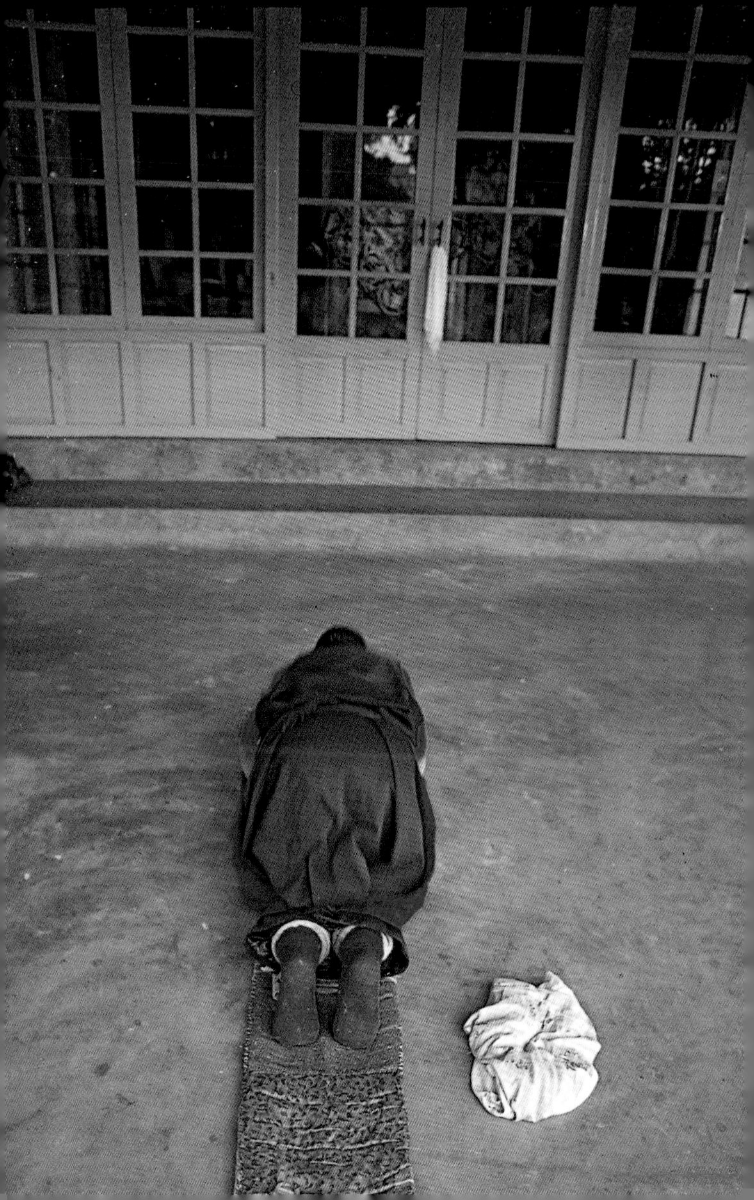

■ Bowing is characteristic of Eastern cultures.

To bow is to lay down your burden in a spirit of surrender before whoever is your refuge. During the Buddha's time, monks took refuge in the Buddha, the sangha, and the middle path.

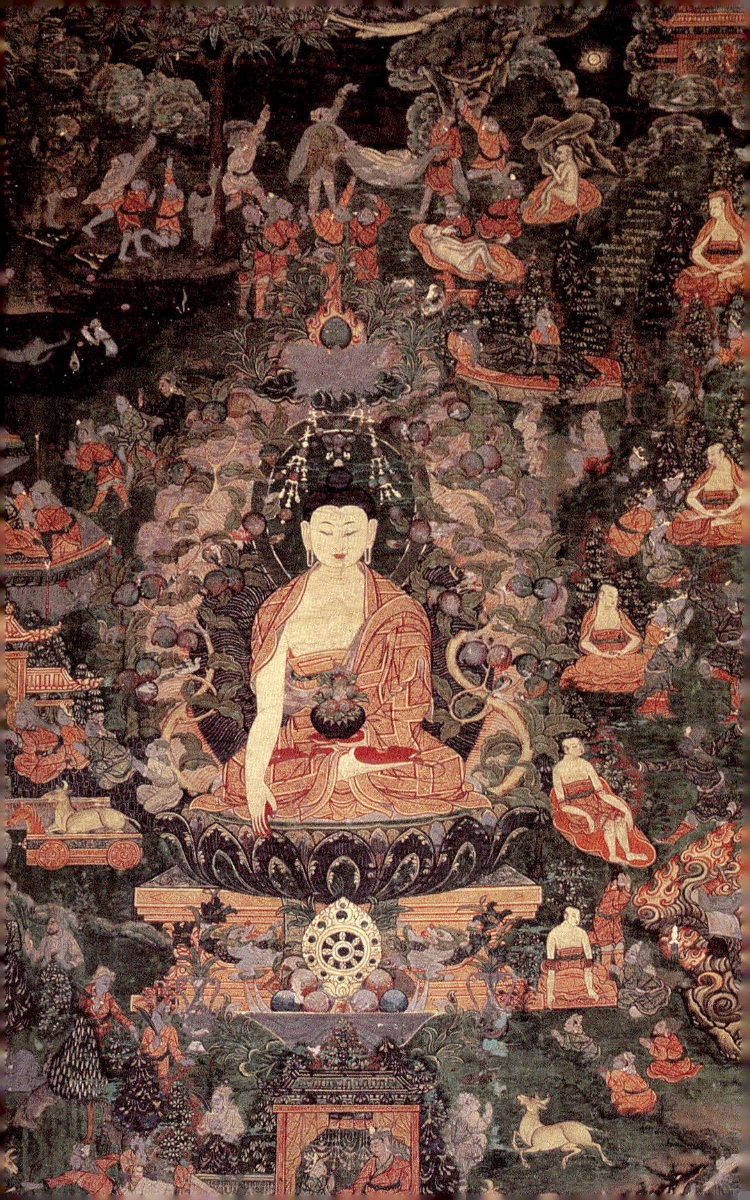

■ May the Earth bear witness

As the meditating Buddha approached enlightenment, Mara, the personification of the forces of Maya, *tempted him. The Buddha touched the ground with his right hand, the palm turned inwards, invoking the earth to bear witness to his good deeds.*

■ *Back cover:* The Buddha and his two disciples

■ *Front cover:* The Enlightened One

■ *Pages 2-3:* A depiction of the Buddha in his various postures

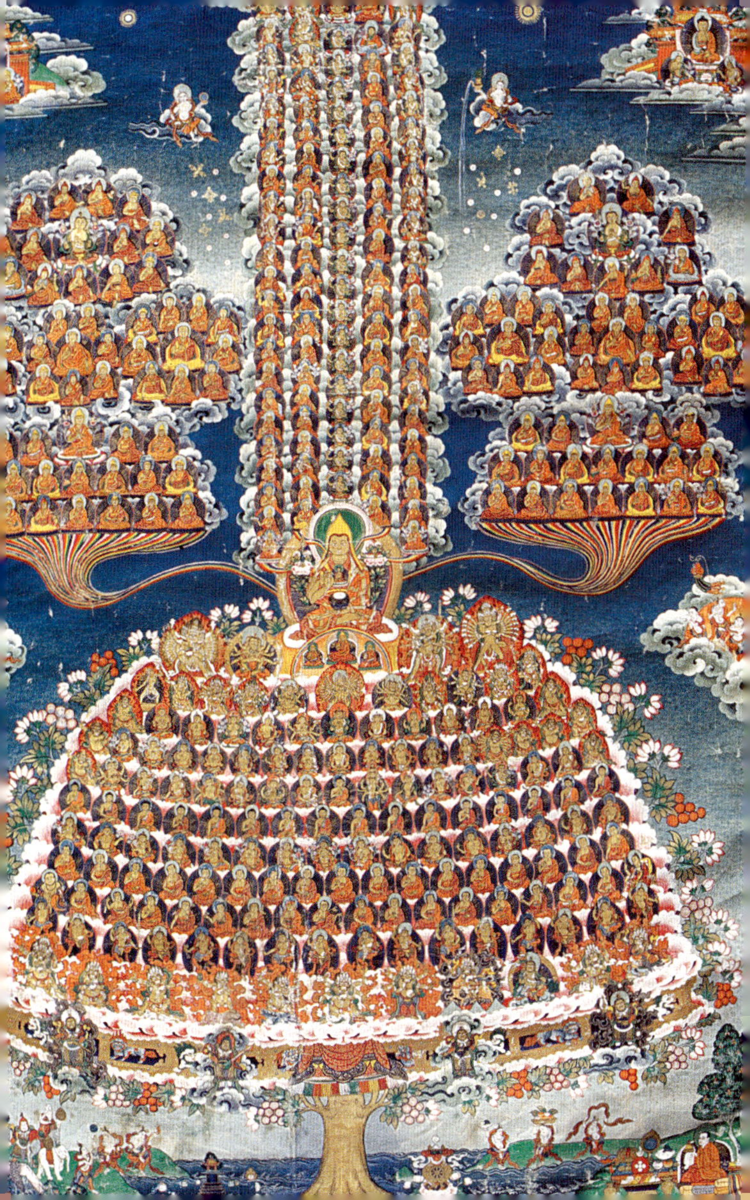

■ The Gelugpa Assembly Tree

The Gelugpa (Yellow Hat) Order is one of the four orders of Buddhism, the one to which the Dalai Lama belongs. The founder of this Order, Tsong-kha-pa, is at the centre of the depiction.